DUBAI TRAVEL GUIDE 2024-2025:

Exploring Dubai's Cultural Heritage

BY

JONATHAN FOSS

TABLE OF CONTENTS

INTRODUCTION 4

    Why Visit Dubai? 10

CHAPTER 1: DISCOVERING DUBAI'S RICH HISTORY......................................17

    Dubai's Ancient Origins............................17

    The Rise of Modern Dubai 23

    Preserving Dubai's Cultural Heritage 29

CHAPTER 2: EXPLORING DUBAI'S ARCHITECTURAL MARVELS 35

    Iconic Skyscrapers and Landmarks 35

    Traditional and Contemporary Architecture.42

    A Glimpse into Future Architectural Projects 49

CHAPTER 3: EMBRACING DUBAI'S DIVERSE CULTURE...................................55

    Multicultural Dubai: A Melting Pot...........55

    Art and Culture Festivals 62

    Emirati Traditions and Customs 68

CHAPTER 4: SAVORING DUBAI'S

CULINARY DELIGHTS.............................**74**

   Culinary Fusion: Dubai's Food Scene........74

   Top Restaurants and Street Food 80

   A Taste of Traditional Emirati Cuisine......91

CHAPTER 5: DUBAI'S NATURAL WONDERS AND OUTDOOR ADVENTURES 98

   Desert Safari and Dune Bashing................98

   Dubai's Pristine Beaches..........................105

   Nature Reserves and Parks.......................111

CHAPTER 6: NAVIGATING DUBAI: PRACTICAL TIPS AND RESOURCES ..117

   Transportation and Getting Around.........117

   Accommodations for Every Budget.........126

   Essential Travel Tips and Resources 133

CONCLUSION **141**

INTRODUCTION

In a world that never ceases to amaze with its myriad wonders, Dubai stands as an indomitable testament to human ambition and innovation. The shimmering jewel of the United Arab Emirates, this desert oasis has evolved at a breakneck pace, transforming itself into a global metropolis that seamlessly blends tradition with modernity. Welcome to the "Dubai Travel Guide 2024-2025: Exploring Dubai's Cultural Heritage" – a journey into a city that is not only a marvel of modern engineering but also a repository of centuries-old traditions and a rich tapestry of cultures.

Dubai, often described as the "City of Gold" or the "Pearl of the Gulf," has garnered global attention for its awe-inspiring skyscrapers, extravagant luxury, and world-class shopping. Yet, beneath the glitz and glamour lies a city deeply rooted in its heritage, where history and modernity coexist harmoniously. It is this fascinating dichotomy that we aim to explore in our comprehensive guide, as we invite you to embark on an unforgettable journey through the heart and soul of Dubai.

As we turn the pages of this book, we will unravel the enigmatic charm of Dubai's cultural heritage, uncovering the stories of its people, its traditions, and its enduring commitment to preserving its past while soaring towards the future. Dubai is not just a city; it is a microcosm of the world, where individuals from diverse backgrounds converge, contributing to its rich cultural mosaic. Through meticulous research, captivating narratives, and stunning visuals, we endeavor to present a kaleidoscopic view of this remarkable city.

Our journey will take us through the labyrinthine alleyways of the historic Al Fahidi Neighborhood, where the gentle whispers of the wind echo tales of a bygone era. We will immerse ourselves in the aromas and flavors of the bustling spice souks, where ancient traditions come alive in the vibrant colors and fragrances that fill the air. We will gaze in awe at the architectural marvels of the past, like the Dubai Creek, the Al Bastakiya district, and the Dubai Museum, while simultaneously witnessing the bold, futuristic skyline that defines contemporary Dubai.

This book is not just a guide; it is an invitation to explore, discover, and experience Dubai in a way that transcends the superficial tourist experience. Whether you are a seasoned traveler seeking new perspectives or a first-time visitor eager to uncover the hidden gems of this extraordinary city, "Dubai Travel Guide 2024-

2025: Exploring Dubai's Cultural Heritage" promises to be your trusted companion.

We have meticulously curated the best experiences, insider tips, and cultural insights to ensure that your journey through Dubai is as enriching as it is exhilarating. From the serene majesty of the desert dunes to the exhilarating adventures of theme parks and water parks, from the traditional Bedouin hospitality to the world-class culinary delights, this guide is your key to unlocking the secrets of Dubai's enchanting blend of old and new.

Prepare to be captivated, intrigued, and inspired as we embark on a voyage through the pages of this book. Dubai, with its endless possibilities and timeless traditions, awaits your exploration. Welcome to "Dubai Travel Guide 2024-2025:

Exploring Dubai's Cultural Heritage." Your adventure begins now.

Why Visit Dubai?

Dubai, a city synonymous with opulence and innovation, stands as a shining gem in the heart of the Middle East. Renowned for its dazzling skyscrapers, luxurious lifestyle, and unique blend of tradition and modernity, Dubai has become a global travel destination like no other. In this book, we explore the compelling reasons why Dubai should be on every traveler's bucket list.

Iconic Architecture:

Dubai's skyline is a testament to human ingenuity and ambition. The city boasts architectural marvels such as the Burj Khalifa, the world's tallest building, and the Palm Jumeirah, an artificial island shaped like a palm tree. These structures not only serve as feats of engineering but also provide breathtaking views and experiences for visitors.

Cultural Diversity:

Dubai is a melting pot of cultures, with residents hailing from over 200 nationalities. This cultural diversity is reflected in the city's vibrant culinary scene, where you can savor dishes from all corners of the globe. Additionally, Dubai hosts numerous cultural festivals, exhibitions, and events that celebrate its multiculturalism, offering travelers a chance to immerse themselves in the world's various traditions.

Luxury Shopping:

Dubai is a shopping paradise, featuring some of the world's most extravagant malls and boutiques. The city is renowned for its tax-free shopping, offering visitors an opportunity to purchase high-end fashion, jewelry, electronics, and more at competitive prices. The Dubai Mall, for instance, is not just a shopping destination but an entertainment hub with an indoor ice rink and an aquarium.

Desert Adventures:

Beyond the glitz and glamour, Dubai's vast desert landscape offers travelers a unique opportunity to experience the tranquility and beauty of the Arabian desert. Desert safaris, dune bashing, camel rides, and starlit dinners in Bedouin-style camps are just some of the activities that allow you to explore the mesmerizing desert scenery.

Thriving Nightlife:

Dubai's nightlife is legendary, with a plethora of world-class nightclubs, bars, and lounges. Many establishments feature renowned DJs and live entertainment, creating an electric atmosphere that keeps the city alive well into the night. Whether you're looking to dance the night away or enjoy a relaxing cocktail with a view, Dubai's nightlife caters to all tastes.

Family-Friendly Attractions:

Dubai is a fantastic destination for families. It offers a wide range of family-friendly attractions such as theme parks like Dubai Parks and Resorts, water parks like Atlantis Aquaventure, and indoor entertainment centers like IMG Worlds of Adventure. The city also hosts educational attractions like Dubai Aquarium and

Underwater Zoo, making it an ideal destination for family vacations.

Safety and Cleanliness:

Dubai is renowned for its safety and cleanliness. The city consistently ranks among the safest places to visit in the world. With strict law enforcement, low crime rates, and impeccable cleanliness, travelers can explore Dubai with peace of mind.

Dubai's unique blend of modernity, culture, luxury, and adventure make it an unparalleled destination for travelers from all walks of life. Whether you're a thrill-seeker, a shopaholic, a culture enthusiast, or a family looking for a memorable vacation, Dubai offers something for everyone. With its iconic skyline, diverse culinary scene, and endless entertainment options, Dubai continues to captivate the world and remains a must-visit destination for those seeking an unforgettable travel experience. So, pack your bags and get ready to explore the jewel of the Middle East – Dubai.

CHAPTER 1: DISCOVERING DUBAI'S RICH HISTORY

Dubai's Ancient Origins

Dubai, a global metropolis renowned for its modernity and opulence, has a history that traces its roots back to ancient times. Beneath the glittering skyscrapers and bustling streets lies a fascinating tale of human civilization and resilience. In this article, we delve into the enigmatic origins of Dubai, shedding light on the city's ancient past and the historical factors that have shaped it into the vibrant hub it is today.

The Birth of Dubai:

Dubai's history can be traced back over 4,000 years when it was primarily a fishing and trading settlement on the shores of the Persian Gulf. The city's strategic location at the crossroads of ancient trade routes made it an attractive destination for traders and merchants from as early as the Bronze Age. Archaeological excavations have revealed artifacts from as far back as the 3rd millennium BC, providing evidence of Dubai's existence during ancient times.

Trade and Prosperity:

One of the defining aspects of Dubai's ancient origins was its role as a vital trading center. The city served as a link between the civilizations of Mesopotamia and the Indus Valley, facilitating the exchange of goods such as pearls, spices, textiles, and precious metals. The renowned Incense Route, connecting the Arabian Peninsula to the Mediterranean, passed through Dubai, further enhancing its importance in the ancient world.

Pearl Diving:

Before the discovery of oil, Dubai's economy was predominantly reliant on pearl diving. From the late 19th century until the mid-20th century, pearl diving was a major industry that sustained the city's population. The prized pearls harvested from the Persian Gulf's oyster beds were sought after by traders and nobility across the globe. Dubai's pearl diving heritage is a testament to the resilience and maritime prowess of its ancient inhabitants.

The Trucial States:

Throughout its history, Dubai, along with several neighboring emirates, was part of a confederation known as the Trucial States. These emirates, including Abu Dhabi, Sharjah, and Ras Al Khaimah, were collectively responsible for maintaining stability in the region and safeguarding trade routes. The British established treaties with the Trucial States in the 19th century, which provided a degree of protection and influence that shaped the emirates' modern development.

The Transformation:

Dubai's transformation from a humble fishing village to a global economic powerhouse is nothing short of remarkable. While its ancient origins laid the groundwork for its role in trade and commerce, it was the discovery of oil in the 20th century that catapulted Dubai into the modern era. With visionary leadership, Dubai invested oil revenues into infrastructure, diversification of the economy, and the development of world-class amenities, making it an international hub for finance, trade, tourism, and culture.

Dubai's ancient origins are a testament to the resilience, adaptability, and entrepreneurial spirit of its people. From its humble beginnings as a fishing village to its current status as a global metropolis, the city has undergone an extraordinary transformation. Understanding the rich tapestry of Dubai's ancient history provides valuable insights into the factors that have contributed to its prosperity and growth. Today, Dubai stands as a symbol of human ingenuity and a bridge between the ancient and the modern, offering a glimpse into the enduring legacy of its past.

The Rise of Modern Dubai

Dubai, once a humble fishing village nestled along the shores of the Arabian Gulf, has transformed into a global icon of modernity, luxury, and innovation. The rise of modern Dubai is a testament to the visionary leadership, strategic planning, and relentless pursuit of excellence that has propelled this city to international acclaim. In this article, we will explore the remarkable journey of Dubai's evolution into a modern metropolis.

Visionary Leadership:

The foundation of Dubai's transformation was laid by the visionary leadership of its rulers, particularly His Highness Sheikh Rashid bin Saeed Al Maktoum and His Highness Sheikh Mohammed bin Rashid Al Maktoum. These leaders envisioned Dubai as a global hub for trade, tourism, and finance, and their unwavering commitment to this vision has been the driving force behind the city's progress.

Strategic Location:

Dubai's strategic location, situated at the crossroads of Europe, Asia, and Africa, made it a natural trading hub for centuries. However, it was the city's leadership that leveraged this geographic advantage to turn Dubai into a logistical and transportation powerhouse. The development of the Jebel Ali Port and the Dubai International Airport played pivotal roles in facilitating global trade and tourism.

Infrastructure Development:

One of the most striking aspects of modern Dubai is its awe-inspiring infrastructure. The city boasts a skyline punctuated by iconic structures like the Burj Khalifa, the world's tallest building, and the Palm Jumeirah, a man-made island visible from space. These architectural marvels have not only reshaped the city's landscape but have also attracted global attention and investment.

Economic Diversification:

Dubai's early reliance on oil revenue prompted leaders to seek economic diversification. The establishment of free zones, such as the Dubai International Financial Centre (DIFC) and Dubai Media City, transformed the city into a business-friendly environment, fostering entrepreneurship, innovation, and foreign investment.

Tourism and Hospitality:

Dubai's transformation into a global tourism hotspot is nothing short of remarkable. With world-class hotels, entertainment options, and year-round sunshine, the city has become a magnet for tourists from across the globe. The Dubai Mall, an epicenter of shopping and leisure, and the Burj Al Arab, often hailed as the world's most luxurious hotel, exemplify the city's commitment to hospitality.

Cultural Diversity:

Modern Dubai is a melting pot of cultures and nationalities. A liberal approach to immigration has attracted a diverse expatriate community, contributing to the city's cosmopolitan character.

This cultural fusion has enriched Dubai's culinary, artistic, and social landscapes.

Sustainability and Innovation:

As Dubai looks towards the future, sustainability has become a key focus. Initiatives like the Dubai Clean Energy Strategy 2050 aim to make Dubai a global leader in clean energy. The city is also exploring innovative technologies, such as the Hyperloop and autonomous vehicles, to further enhance its infrastructure and transportation systems.

The rise of modern Dubai is a captivating narrative of transformation, ambition, and resilience. From a humble desert outpost to a global hub of commerce, culture, and luxury, Dubai's journey is a testament to the power of visionary leadership, strategic planning, and unwavering determination. As the city continues to evolve, it serves as an inspiration to cities around the world, demonstrating that with a clear vision and unwavering commitment to progress, the sky is not the limit – it's just the beginning.

Preserving Dubai's Cultural Heritage

Dubai, a thriving metropolis on the southeastern coast of the Arabian Peninsula, has transformed itself into a global economic and cultural hub over the past few decades. Amidst the skyscrapers, luxury resorts, and modern infrastructure, Dubai remains deeply committed to preserving its rich cultural heritage. This commitment reflects not only the city's respect for its past but also its vision for a harmonious future where tradition and progress coexist. In this article, we delve into the efforts made by Dubai to preserve its cultural heritage and why this endeavor is crucial in maintaining its unique identity.

Significance:

Dubai's roots as a trading and fishing village date back centuries. Its strategic location along historic trade routes contributed to a rich tapestry of cultures and traditions that have left an indelible mark on the city. To preserve this heritage, Dubai has undertaken several initiatives:

a. Al Fahidi Historical Neighborhood: The Al Fahidi Historical Neighborhood, also known as

Al Bastakiya, is a restored district showcasing traditional Emirati architecture. It offers visitors a glimpse into Dubai's past with its narrow lanes, wind towers, and heritage houses.

b. Dubai Museum: Housed in the historic Al Fahidi Fort, the Dubai Museum provides an immersive experience into the city's history, showcasing artifacts and exhibits that highlight its journey from a small fishing village to a global metropolis.

Cultural Celebrations:
Dubai takes pride in celebrating its cultural diversity through a variety of events and festivals:

a. Dubai Shopping Festival: This annual event celebrates traditional Emirati craftsmanship, offering visitors the chance to purchase locally-made goods and experience traditional Emirati hospitality.

b. Dubai Food Festival: A culinary extravaganza that celebrates both local and international cuisine, showcasing the rich culinary traditions of the region.

Architectural Marvels:
Dubai's commitment to preserving its heritage is also evident in its architectural endeavors:

a. Dubai Opera: While being a modern marvel, the Dubai Opera pays homage to traditional Arabic design elements. Its dhow-shaped structure and attention to detail evoke the city's maritime history.

b. Dubai Frame: The Dubai Frame is a colossal architectural feat that provides panoramic views of the old and new Dubai, symbolically framing the city's past and future.

Initiatives to Safeguard Heritage:

Dubai has established various organizations and initiatives to ensure the preservation of its cultural heritage:

a. Dubai Culture & Arts Authority: This government entity is dedicated to promoting cultural awareness and supporting heritage preservation projects across the city.

b. Dubai Heritage Development: This organization is actively involved in the restoration and maintenance of historical sites and landmarks, ensuring that they remain accessible to both residents and tourists.

Dubai's commitment to preserving its cultural heritage demonstrates its deep respect for tradition and a profound understanding of the importance of preserving its unique identity. In doing so, Dubai manages to strike a delicate balance between embracing progress and honoring its roots. As the city continues to evolve, it serves as a shining example of how a modern metropolis can cherish its cultural heritage while charting a path towards a prosperous future. By celebrating its past, Dubai remains not only a global economic powerhouse but also a custodian of its rich cultural legacy for generations to come.

CHAPTER 2: EXPLORING DUBAI'S ARCHITECTURAL MARVELS

Iconic Skyscrapers and Landmarks

Dubai, a city known for its opulence and grandeur, is a true testament to human ingenuity in architectural design and construction. Nestled in the heart of the United Arab Emirates, Dubai has rapidly transformed from a humble desert outpost to a global metropolis adorned with iconic skyscrapers and landmarks that defy imagination. In this exploration of Dubai's architectural marvels, we will embark on a journey through the cityscape that showcases not only the architectural prowess but also the cultural and economic dynamism of this remarkable city.

Burj Khalifa: Touching the Sky

Our journey begins with the crown jewel of Dubai's skyline, the Burj Khalifa. Standing at a staggering 828 meters (2,717 feet), this iconic skyscraper is not only the tallest building in the world but also a symbol of Dubai's ambition and vision. Designed by Adrian Smith of the architectural firm SOM, the Burj Khalifa is a true engineering marvel, boasting a stunning fusion of Islamic and modern design elements.

Visitors to the Burj Khalifa can take an exhilarating journey to the observation deck on the 148th floor, where breathtaking panoramic views of the cityscape and the Arabian Gulf await. As you stand at this dizzying height, you'll gain a profound appreciation for the audaciousness of human achievement in architecture and construction.

The Palm Jumeirah: Man-Made Wonder

From the sky-piercing heights of the Burj Khalifa, we descend to explore one of Dubai's most iconic man-made wonders - The Palm Jumeirah. Shaped like a palm tree and extending into the Persian Gulf, this artificial island is an engineering marvel that has captured the world's imagination. Conceived by Nakheel Properties, The Palm Jumeirah is a testament to Dubai's ambition to push the boundaries of urban planning.

The island is home to luxurious resorts, villas, and a stunning array of entertainment and leisure options. A walk along the crescent-shaped boardwalk provides a unique perspective of the city, as you gaze upon the glittering skyline while the waves lap gently at the shore.

The Dubai Mall: Where Shopping Meets Architecture

While Dubai is known for its awe-inspiring skyscrapers, it also boasts architectural marvels on a smaller scale. The Dubai Mall is a prime example of this fusion of commerce and design. Located at the base of the Burj Khalifa, it is not just a shopping destination but a destination in itself.

Designed by DP Architects, The Dubai Mall encompasses more than just retail outlets. It features a dazzling indoor ice rink, an enormous aquarium, and a captivating waterfall. The mall's interior is a symphony of natural light, water features, and contemporary design, making it a must-visit destination for architecture enthusiasts and shoppers alike.

Burj Al Arab: The Sail of Luxury

Our architectural journey in Dubai would be incomplete without a visit to the iconic Burj Al Arab. Shaped like a billowing sail, this seven-star hotel is a masterpiece of design and engineering by architect Tom Wright. Perched on its own island, the Burj Al Arab redefines luxury and extravagance, offering guests an unparalleled experience.

The interior of the Burj Al Arab is a showcase of opulence and grandeur, with gold leaf embellishments, vibrant colors, and sumptuous furnishings. Its helipad, which has hosted numerous stunts and events, offers breathtaking views of the Arabian Gulf. The Burj Al Arab is not just a hotel; it is a symbol of Dubai's commitment to setting new standards in hospitality and architectural innovation.

Dubai's architectural marvels, from the towering Burj Khalifa to the man-made wonder of The Palm Jumeirah, and from the fusion of shopping and design at The Dubai Mall to the luxurious opulence of the Burj Al Arab, all contribute to the city's reputation as a global architectural hub.

Exploring these iconic skyscrapers and landmarks in Dubai is not merely a journey through concrete and steel but an immersion in the spirit of ambition, innovation, and luxury that defines this remarkable city. Dubai's architectural marvels are a testament to the limitless possibilities of human creativity and engineering, and they invite visitors from around the world to witness the future of architecture in the present day.

Traditional and Contemporary Architecture

Dubai, often referred to as the "City of the Future," is a gleaming metropolis that stands as a testament to human ambition and innovation. Its skyline boasts some of the world's most iconic and awe-inspiring architectural wonders. These architectural marvels seamlessly blend traditional design elements with contemporary innovation, creating a unique tapestry that tells the story of Dubai's rapid transformation from a humble desert town to a global economic powerhouse.

Traditional Architecture: A Glimpse into Dubai's Past

Dubai's architectural heritage is deeply rooted in its history as a trading hub along ancient trade routes. Traditional Emirati architecture reflects the region's harsh desert environment, offering both practicality and aesthetics.

Wind Tower Architecture

One of the most recognizable features of traditional Emirati architecture is the wind tower, known as "Barjeel" in Arabic. These tall, slender structures capture the natural breezes and channel them into buildings, providing a natural form of air conditioning. Wind towers are adorned with intricate latticework designs, showcasing the region's craftsmanship.

Courtyard Houses

Courtyard houses, also known as "Arish" houses, are another hallmark of traditional Emirati architecture. These houses are built around a central open courtyard, providing privacy, shade, and ventilation. The intricate wooden detailing and decorative elements on these houses reflect the region's rich artistic heritage.

Contemporary Architecture: Pushing the Boundaries

Dubai's rapid economic growth has given rise to a wave of contemporary architectural masterpieces that have captured the world's imagination. These structures incorporate cutting-edge technology, sustainable design principles, and audacious creativity.

Burj Khalifa

The Burj Khalifa, the world's tallest building, stands as the crown jewel of Dubai's skyline. Designed by Adrian Smith from the architectural firm of Skidmore, Owings & Merrill, this towering structure reaches a staggering height of 828 meters. Its sleek, tapering form is inspired by traditional Islamic architecture, with a spiraling minaret-like design that reflects the city's cultural heritage.

Palm Jumeirah

Palm Jumeirah is an artificial island that takes the shape of a palm tree and is one of the most iconic examples of Dubai's ingenuity. Designed by Nakheel Properties, this man-made wonder features a combination of luxury residences, hotels, and entertainment options. It is a testament to Dubai's ability to reshape its natural landscape for both aesthetic and functional purposes.

Dubai Opera House

The Dubai Opera House is a contemporary architectural gem that showcases the city's commitment to culture and the arts. Designed by Atkins, the building's sleek, futuristic design is inspired by the shape of a traditional dhow, a traditional Arabian sailing vessel. It serves as a cultural hub for music, theater, and performing arts.

The Fusion of Tradition and Modernity

What sets Dubai apart is its ability to seamlessly blend traditional and contemporary architectural elements. This fusion can be seen in structures like the Al Fahidi Historic District, where traditional wind towers coexist with modern art galleries, cafes, and boutique hotels. It's a testament to Dubai's respect for its heritage while embracing progress and innovation.

As Dubai continues to evolve, its architectural landscape will undoubtedly continue to captivate the world's imagination. The city's commitment to pushing the boundaries of design and sustainability while preserving its rich heritage is a lesson for cities worldwide. Exploring Dubai's architectural marvels is not just a journey through stunning buildings but also a glimpse into the soul of a city that never ceases to inspire.

In conclusion, Dubai's architectural wonders bridge the gap between the past and the future, offering a rich tapestry of tradition and modernity. They stand as symbols of human ingenuity, innovation, and the relentless pursuit of excellence in architecture. Exploring Dubai's architectural marvels is a journey through time and space, an experience that leaves an indelible mark on anyone fortunate enough to witness it.

A Glimpse into Future Architectural Projects

Dubai, often dubbed the "City of the Future," has long been a global hub for groundbreaking architectural innovation. With its audacious vision, limitless resources, and a commitment to pushing the boundaries of design and technology, Dubai continues to be a beacon for architects and designers worldwide. In this article, we embark on a journey to explore some of the most exciting future architectural projects in Dubai, where imagination knows no limits.

The Dubai Creek Tower

The Dubai Creek Tower is a testament to Dubai's ambition to reach new heights, quite literally. Designed by the renowned architect Santiago Calatrava, this iconic structure is set to surpass the Burj Khalifa, currently the world's tallest building. The tower, which resembles a blossoming lily, symbolizes growth and prosperity. Its observation deck will offer panoramic views of the city, the Arabian Gulf, and beyond. The Dubai Creek Tower is not just an architectural marvel; it's a symbol of Dubai's commitment to achieving the extraordinary.

The Museum of the Future

The Museum of the Future is a testament to Dubai's commitment to technology and innovation. Located in the heart of the city, this museum is more than just a showcase of futuristic gadgets; it's a visionary concept in itself. The building's design, featuring a gleaming oval-shaped structure adorned with Arabic calligraphy, is a fusion of traditional Islamic design and cutting-edge technology.

Inside, visitors can explore exhibits on artificial intelligence, robotics, and sustainability, offering a glimpse into the world of tomorrow.

Aladdin City

Inspired by the tales of Aladdin and the Arabian Nights, Aladdin City is an enchanting architectural project that aims to recreate the mystique of the past in a modern urban setting. The project comprises three towering structures that are interconnected by air-conditioned bridges resembling giant golden lamps. These structures will house commercial and hotel spaces, creating a stunning visual spectacle along Dubai Creek. Aladdin City embodies Dubai's commitment to weaving its rich cultural heritage into contemporary designs.

The Dubai Eye

The Dubai Eye, also known as the Ain Dubai, is set to be the world's largest observation wheel. Located on Bluewaters Island, this colossal structure will offer breathtaking views of the Dubai skyline and the Arabian Gulf. Each glass-enclosed capsule will provide a luxurious experience, combining entertainment and unparalleled vistas. The Dubai Eye is a testament to Dubai's commitment to offering unique and unforgettable experiences to its residents and visitors.

The Floating Venice

The Floating Venice is an architectural concept that takes the luxury resort experience to new heights—or, in this case, new depths. This ambitious project aims to recreate the charm and romance of Venice in the waters of the Arabian Gulf. With underwater suites, gondola rides, and Venetian-style architecture, the Floating Venice promises an otherworldly experience that marries classic European elegance with Dubai's modern opulence.

Dubai's architectural marvels are a testament to its unwavering commitment to innovation, luxury, and pushing the boundaries of what is possible. The future architectural projects discussed in this article are not only ambitious in design and scale but also embody the spirit of Dubai itself—a city that dares to dream big and turns those dreams into reality. As we look ahead to the completion of these projects, we can only imagine the new heights to which Dubai's architectural prowess will ascend, further solidifying its reputation as a city of the future.

CHAPTER 3:
EMBRACING DUBAI'S
DIVERSE CULTURE

Multicultural Dubai: A Melting Pot

Dubai, the dazzling jewel of the United Arab Emirates, is renowned for its towering skyscrapers, luxurious lifestyles, and as a global hub for business and tourism. However, beyond its opulent exterior lies a rich tapestry of diverse cultures that have converged to create a truly unique and harmonious multicultural society. In this article, we will explore how Dubai has embraced and celebrated its diverse culture, establishing itself as a true melting pot of the world.

A Global Melting Pot:

Dubai's multiculturalism is a testament to its strategic geographical location, serving as a bridge between the East and the West. Over the decades, the city has attracted expatriates and professionals from every corner of the globe, creating a vibrant and dynamic population. The UAE government's open-door policy has played a significant role in welcoming people of various nationalities, cultures, and backgrounds.

A Microcosm of the World:

Dubai's population is a microcosm of the world's diversity. Expatriates from Asia, Europe, Africa, and the Americas call this city their home. This diversity is reflected not only in its residents but also in the wide array of languages spoken, cuisines available, and traditions practiced. It's not uncommon to hear Arabic, English, Hindi, Urdu, Tagalog, and more being spoken on the streets of Dubai.

Cultural Celebrations and Festivals:

Dubai takes pride in celebrating the traditions and festivals of its diverse residents. From Diwali to Eid, Christmas to Chinese New Year, Dubai hosts a multitude of cultural festivals and events throughout the year. These celebrations not only provide a sense of belonging for the expatriate communities but also offer locals an opportunity to learn and appreciate different customs and practices.

Culinary Diversity:

One of the most delightful aspects of Dubai's multiculturalism is its culinary scene. The city boasts a culinary landscape that spans the globe, offering an incredible array of international cuisines. From street food stalls to Michelin-starred restaurants, Dubai's dining options cater to every palate. Embracing the diverse culinary traditions has not only enriched the city's gastronomic offerings but has also encouraged cultural exchange through food.

Cultural Centers and Museums:

Dubai has invested in cultural centers and museums that celebrate its multicultural identity. The Etihad Museum, Dubai Opera, and Al Fahidi Historic Neighborhood are just a few examples of places where visitors can explore the history and heritage of the UAE and its diverse population. These institutions contribute to fostering an environment of cultural appreciation and understanding.

Tolerance and Inclusivity:

The UAE government places a strong emphasis on tolerance and inclusivity, which is enshrined in its policies and vision for the nation. The "Year of Tolerance" in 2019 was a testament to the country's commitment to fostering a harmonious society where people of all backgrounds can coexist peacefully.

Dubai's embrace of its diverse culture is not merely a marketing slogan but a lived reality.

The city has successfully woven the threads of various cultures into its social fabric, creating a tapestry of harmony, acceptance, and prosperity. As Dubai continues to grow and evolve, its multicultural spirit remains a beacon of hope and an example for the world to follow. In the heart of the desert, Dubai has truly become a global melting pot, a place where the world comes together in unity and celebration of its rich diversity.

Art and Culture Festivals

Dubai, a vibrant and cosmopolitan city in the heart of the United Arab Emirates, is known for its breathtaking skyscrapers, luxurious lifestyle, and thriving business hub. However, beyond its modern façade lies a rich tapestry of diverse cultures that have come together to create a unique blend of traditions, beliefs, and art forms. One of the most profound ways Dubai celebrates and showcases this diversity is through its numerous art and culture festivals. These festivals serve as a bridge that connects different cultures, fostering unity, understanding, and appreciation for the myriad of traditions that call Dubai home.

Celebrating Diversity

Dubai's cultural landscape is a mosaic of nationalities, with expatriates comprising a significant portion of its population. The city's art and culture festivals are a reflection of this diversity. Whether it's the Dubai International Film Festival, the Dubai Food Festival, or the Dubai Jazz Festival, these events bring together artists, chefs, musicians, and performers from around the world, allowing residents and visitors to experience and appreciate different cultural expressions.

Promoting Tolerance

Tolerance is a core value of Dubai's vision for the future. The art and culture festivals play a pivotal role in promoting tolerance by showcasing the beauty and uniqueness of various cultural traditions. These festivals are a testament to Dubai's commitment to creating an inclusive and harmonious society where people of all backgrounds can coexist peacefully.

Fostering Cultural Exchange

Dubai's art and culture festivals provide a platform for cultural exchange. Through art exhibitions, workshops, and performances, people from diverse backgrounds can engage in meaningful dialogue, learn from each other, and celebrate their differences. Such interactions foster a deeper understanding of different cultures and help break down stereotypes and prejudices.

Preserving Heritage

While Dubai is known for its modernity, it also recognizes the importance of preserving its cultural heritage. Many festivals in the city include elements of Emirati culture, from traditional music and dance to local cuisine. These festivals serve as a means of passing down traditions to the younger generation and ensuring that Emirati culture remains vibrant and relevant.

Economic Impact

Art and culture festivals in Dubai also have a significant economic impact. They attract tourists from around the world, boosting the hospitality, retail, and tourism sectors. Additionally, these festivals provide opportunities for local artists, artisans, and entrepreneurs to showcase their talent and products, contributing to the city's economy.

The Dubai Expo 2020 Effect

The Dubai Expo 2020, which has been extended to 2022, is another testament to Dubai's commitment to celebrating diversity. The Expo brings together countries from all over the world to showcase their culture, innovation, and achievements. It serves as a global stage where visitors can explore and appreciate the richness of cultures from around the globe.

Dubai's art and culture festivals are more than just entertainment; they are a testament to the city's commitment to embracing its diverse cultural tapestry. Through these festivals, Dubai promotes tolerance, fosters cultural exchange, and celebrates its unique blend of traditions. As the city continues to evolve, these festivals will play a crucial role in preserving its heritage while shaping a more inclusive and harmonious future. Dubai's art and culture festivals are a true reflection of the city's spirit and its dedication to fostering unity in diversity.

Emirati Traditions and Customs

Dubai, the dazzling gem of the United Arab Emirates, is a city known for its remarkable skyscrapers, luxury lifestyle, and a rich tapestry of cultures coexisting harmoniously. At the heart of this multicultural mosaic are the Emirati traditions and customs that have played a pivotal role in shaping Dubai's identity. In this article, we will explore the rich heritage of Emirati traditions and customs, highlighting how they have evolved and coalesced with the diverse cultures present in Dubai today.

The Bedouin Heritage: A Foundation of Emirati Culture

The roots of Emirati culture can be traced back to the Bedouin nomads who inhabited the Arabian Peninsula for centuries. These resilient desert-dwellers have left an indelible mark on the Emirati way of life. Key aspects of their heritage, such as hospitality, loyalty, and a deep connection to the desert, continue to be central to Emirati traditions.

Emirati Hospitality: A Warm Welcome to All

Emiratis are renowned for their exceptional hospitality. Guests are considered a blessing, and it is a point of pride for Emiratis to provide a warm welcome to visitors. This custom is deeply ingrained in the culture, with traditional coffee (gahwa) and dates being offered as a gesture of goodwill. Emirati households often have a majlis, a designated space for receiving guests, where conversations flow freely and guests are treated with utmost respect.

Emirati Dress: Tradition Meets Modernity

The traditional Emirati attire reflects the blend of tradition and modernity in Dubai. While Western-style clothing is common in daily life, Emiratis take great pride in wearing their traditional dress on special occasions. For men, this typically includes the kandura, a flowing white robe, while women wear the abaya, often beautifully embellished. The headscarf (ghutra for men and sheyla for women) is also an integral part of the traditional attire.

Celebrating Islamic Festivals

Islam is the predominant religion in Dubai, and Islamic festivals hold great significance in Emirati culture. Ramadan, Eid al-Fitr, and Eid al-Adha are celebrated with fervor and unity. During Ramadan, Muslims fast from sunrise to sunset, and communal iftars (breaking of the fast) bring people from all backgrounds together. The spirit of giving is exemplified through zakat (charity) during this holy month.

Emirati Cuisine: A Culinary Journey

Emirati cuisine offers a delectable fusion of flavors influenced by various cultures that have touched the region over centuries. Traditional dishes like al harees (wheat and meat porridge) and al majboos (spiced rice with meat) are savored alongside international cuisine in Dubai's diverse culinary landscape. The food reflects the multicultural harmony that defines the city.

Embracing Diversity: Dubai's Multiculturalism

Dubai is a melting pot of cultures from all corners of the globe. Emiratis have embraced this diversity with open arms, promoting tolerance and coexistence. It is not uncommon to see Emiratis participating in celebrations of various cultures, be it Diwali, Christmas, or Chinese New Year. The city's ethos is encapsulated in the slogan "Unity in Diversity."

Sustainability and Innovation

As Dubai continues to evolve, it is committed to preserving its traditions while embracing the future. Sustainability and innovation are integral parts of the Emirati vision. The city's commitment to renewable energy, cultural preservation, and sustainable development showcases its forward-thinking approach.

Embracing Dubai's diverse culture is a testament to the enduring traditions and customs of the Emirati people. These customs, deeply rooted in the Bedouin heritage, have adapted and thrived in the face of modernization and globalization. Dubai's remarkable blend of cultures, marked by its hospitality, cuisine, and celebration of diversity, underscores its status as a global city while paying homage to its Emirati roots. In this dynamic cultural mosaic, Dubai stands as a shining example of how traditions and modernity can coexist harmoniously in a vibrant, cosmopolitan setting.

CHAPTER 4: SAVORING DUBAI'S CULINARY DELIGHTS

Culinary Fusion: Dubai's Food Scene

Dubai, known for its opulence and extravagance, is a city that has rapidly evolved into a global culinary destination. With its diverse population and a strong emphasis on innovation and luxury, Dubai's food scene has become a true melting pot of flavors and cultures. At the heart of this vibrant culinary tapestry lies the art of culinary fusion, where traditional recipes meet modern techniques and international influences. In this article, we will delve into the world of culinary fusion in Dubai and explore how it has contributed to the city's reputation as a food lover's paradise.

The Cultural Mosaic of Dubai

Dubai's food scene mirrors its multicultural population. The city is home to a diverse mix of nationalities, with expatriates from all corners of the world. This cultural mosaic has resulted in a rich and varied culinary landscape, where you can find authentic dishes from India, Pakistan, Lebanon, Egypt, Japan, Italy, and beyond.

However, what truly sets Dubai apart is its ability to seamlessly blend these culinary traditions to create something entirely new and exciting.

The Art of Culinary Fusion

Culinary fusion, as an art form, is the harmonious blending of different culinary traditions, ingredients, and techniques. In Dubai, this art is practiced with finesse and creativity, resulting in dishes that are not only delicious but also visually stunning. Here are a few examples of how culinary fusion manifests in Dubai's food scene:

- Emirati Meets International: Emirati cuisine, rooted in the traditions of the Arabian Peninsula, has embraced international influences. Dishes like camel burgers with truffle aioli or saffron-infused risotto with Gulf seafood showcase the city's ability to blend local flavors with global appeal.

- East Meets West: Dubai is known for its upscale dining experiences, and many restaurants incorporate elements from both Eastern and Western cuisines. Sushi burritos, kebab tacos, and Arabic-inspired pasta dishes are just a few examples of how these worlds collide on a plate.

- Fusion Desserts: Dubai's pastry chefs have taken dessert to a whole new level with fusion creations like date-filled croissants, baklava cheesecake, and cardamom-infused chocolate truffles. These delightful treats bring together the best of local and international confectionery.

- Street Food Reimagined: Dubai's street food vendors have elevated traditional dishes to gourmet status. Shawarma-inspired tacos, falafel sliders, and gourmet hot dogs with Middle Eastern toppings are some of the mouthwatering street food offerings you'll find in the city.

The Role of Luxury Dining

Dubai's culinary fusion is not limited to street food and casual eateries. The city's fine dining establishments also play a pivotal role in pushing the boundaries of gastronomy. Michelin-starred chefs from around the world have opened restaurants in Dubai, where they experiment with local ingredients and global influences. This fusion of haute cuisine and traditional flavors has resulted in extraordinary tasting menus and dining experiences that are unparalleled.

Dubai's food scene, characterized by its culinary fusion, has evolved into a remarkable reflection of the city's cosmopolitan spirit. Savoring Dubai's culinary delights is not just about tasting exceptional food; it's about experiencing the innovation, creativity, and cultural harmony that define this dynamic city. Whether you're exploring the bustling streets or indulging in a Michelin-starred feast, Dubai's culinary fusion will undoubtedly leave you with a taste of the extraordinary. So, embark on a culinary journey through this thriving metropolis and savor the delightful fusion of flavors that Dubai has to offer.

Top Restaurants and Street Food

Dubai, a city known for its opulence and innovation, is equally famous for its diverse and tantalizing culinary scene. From luxurious dining experiences in world-class restaurants to the humble yet delectable street food stalls, Dubai offers a spectrum of flavors that cater to every palate. In this article, we will explore the top restaurants and street food destinations that should be on your list when savoring Dubai's culinary delights.

Top Restaurants:

Zuma Dubai:

Nestled in the heart of the city, Zuma Dubai offers a contemporary twist on traditional Japanese izakaya dining. With its stylish ambiance, exceptional service, and a menu boasting fresh sushi, sashimi, and robata grill dishes, Zuma is a haven for food connoisseurs.

Pierchic:

For those seeking a truly immersive seafood experience, Pierchic is perched at the end of a pier in the Arabian Gulf. This Michelin-starred restaurant offers stunning panoramic views and a menu featuring the freshest catches of the day.

Nobu Dubai:

Nobu, an iconic Japanese-Peruvian fusion restaurant, has found its Dubai home in the luxurious Atlantis, The Palm. With dishes like black cod miso and yellowtail jalapeño, it's a culinary journey unlike any other.

Al Hadheerah at Bab Al Shams Desert Resort:
Immerse yourself in Arabian culture at Al Hadheerah, where you can enjoy traditional Middle Eastern dishes while watching live entertainment under the desert stars. The ambience and the food make for a magical experience.

Pai Thai:

Located on the banks of the Dubai waterways, Pai Thai offers authentic Thai cuisine in a picturesque setting. From mouthwatering curries to the famous Pad Thai, this restaurant brings the flavors of Thailand to Dubai.

Street Food:

Al Ustad Special Kebab:

Tucked away in the historic district of Bur Dubai, Al Ustad is a legendary Iranian kebab joint. Their succulent lamb kebabs and warm hospitality have been drawing food enthusiasts for decades.

Ravi Restaurant:

Ravi Restaurant is a Dubai institution, celebrated for its Pakistani and North Indian cuisine. The biryanis, butter chicken, and chapli kebabs are not to be missed. It's an affordable gem for those seeking authentic flavors.

Al Mallah Cafeteria:

If you're craving Lebanese street food, head to Al Mallah Cafeteria. Their shawarmas and falafels are iconic in Dubai, and their open-air setting in the bustling Al Diyafah Street adds to the experience.

Logma:

For a taste of Emirati cuisine, visit Logma. They offer traditional dishes like Al Areesh, a date syrup dumpling, and lugaimat, deep-fried dough balls drizzled with date syrup.

The Shawarma Factory:

Shawarma is a staple of Dubai's street food culture, and The Shawarma Factory serves some of the best. Whether you prefer chicken, beef, or lamb, their shawarmas are packed with flavor and always satisfying.

Dubai's culinary scene is a vibrant mosaic of global flavors, where high-end restaurants and humble street food stalls coexist harmoniously. From the extravagance of Michelin-starred dining to the authenticity of street-side delicacies, Dubai offers a gastronomic adventure like no other. So, the next time you find yourself in this remarkable city, be sure to savor Dubai's culinary delights by exploring both its top restaurants and street food gems. Your taste buds will thank you for the journey.

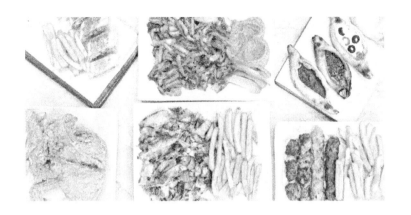

A Taste of Traditional Emirati Cuisine

Dubai, the vibrant and dynamic city in the heart of the United Arab Emirates, is not only known for its towering skyscrapers and luxurious lifestyle but also for its rich culinary heritage. The Emirati cuisine, deeply rooted in tradition and history, offers a sensory journey that takes you through the flavors, aromas, and textures of the Arabian Peninsula. In this exploration of "A Taste of Traditional Emirati Cuisine," we invite you to savor Dubai's culinary delights, a true reflection of the region's culture and heritage.

The Cultural Mosaic of Emirati Cuisine:

Emirati cuisine is a captivating tapestry woven together by centuries of Bedouin, Persian, Indian, and Levantine influences. Its foundation lies in the simplicity of desert living, where ingredients were sourced from the harsh environment. Some key elements of Emirati cuisine include:

- Dates and Coffee: A traditional Emirati welcome includes fresh dates and Arabic coffee (gahwa). The bitterness of the coffee and the sweetness of the dates symbolize the balance of life.

- Seafood: Given Dubai's coastal location, seafood plays a prominent role. Delight in dishes like Sayadiyah (spiced fish with rice) or Harees (slow-cooked wheat and fish).

- Grains and Bread: Bread is central to Emirati cuisine, with Khameer, a sweet, saffron-infused flatbread, being a local favorite. Lugaimat, sweet dough balls soaked in date syrup, are a beloved dessert.

Emirati Cuisine Staples:

Explore the heart of Emirati cuisine with these iconic dishes:

- Al Harees: A slow-cooked dish of wheat and meat, traditionally prepared during Ramadan. It embodies the essence of sharing and community.
- Machboos: A fragrant and spicy rice dish with tender meat, often garnished with nuts and raisins. Variations include chicken, lamb, or fish.
- Al Majboos: A cousin of Machboos, it features prawns or shrimp as the main protein, cooked in a tantalizing blend of spices and rice.

The Spice Trail:

Emirati cuisine is renowned for its exquisite use of spices, showcasing a blend of flavors that captivates the palate. Some of the key spices include saffron, cardamom, cinnamon, and turmeric. These spices not only add depth to the dishes but also offer medicinal properties that have been cherished for generations.

Modern Interpretations:
While Emirati cuisine proudly preserves its traditional roots, Dubai's culinary scene has evolved to include contemporary interpretations. Renowned chefs have taken Emirati flavors and presented them in innovative ways, blending tradition with modernity.

Where to Savor Emirati Cuisine in Dubai:
Dubai offers a plethora of dining options to experience the best of Emirati cuisine. Some notable places to explore include:

- Al Fanar Restaurant and Cafe: A charming venue that transports you to an old Emirati home, offering authentic dishes and a cultural experience.

- Local Markets and Food Stalls: Wander through traditional souks and markets like the Al Fahidi Historical Neighborhood and Al Khabeer Street to sample street food and homemade Emirati dishes.
- Fine Dining Experiences: Upscale restaurants like Seven Sands and Pierchic offer refined Emirati cuisine with stunning views.

Dubai's culinary scene is a testament to the city's commitment to preserving its rich heritage while embracing the global influences that make it a diverse metropolis. A taste of traditional Emirati cuisine is not just a culinary experience; it's a journey through time and culture, an invitation to savor the flavors of the Arabian Peninsula, and a celebration of Dubai's culinary delights. So, the next time you visit this captivating city, make sure to savor the treasures of Emirati cuisine and enrich your culinary journey with its profound history and unique flavors.

CHAPTER 5: DUBAI'S NATURAL WONDERS AND OUTDOOR ADVENTURES

Desert Safari and Dune Bashing

Dubai, known for its modern skyline and luxurious lifestyle, is also home to some of the world's most mesmerizing natural wonders and outdoor adventures. Amidst the towering skyscrapers and opulent hotels lies an enchanting desert landscape that offers a unique blend of tranquility and exhilaration. In this article, we will delve into the captivating world of Desert Safari and Dune Bashing, two exhilarating activities that showcase the rich beauty of Dubai's desert ecosystem while delivering an adrenaline rush like no other.

Dubai's Desert Safari:

A Desert Safari in Dubai is an expedition that allows visitors to immerse themselves in the rugged splendor of the Arabian Desert. The experience begins with a comfortable pick-up from your hotel, setting the stage for a day of adventure and discovery. Here's what you can expect:

- Camel Riding: As you venture deep into the desert, you'll have the opportunity to ride a camel, the 'ship of the desert.' This serene experience allows you to connect with the nomadic heritage of the region while enjoying sweeping views of the endless sand dunes.

- Sandboarding: For thrill-seekers, sandboarding offers an adrenaline-pumping experience. Glide down the dunes on a sandboard, mastering the art of balance and speed as you descend the golden slopes.

- Bedouin Camp: The highlight of a Desert Safari is the visit to a traditional Bedouin camp. Here, you can savor a delicious buffet of Middle Eastern cuisine while taking in a mesmerizing belly dancing performance. The camp also offers opportunities for henna tattooing, shisha smoking, and stargazing.

Dune Bashing in Dubai:

Dune Bashing, also known as Desert Off-Roading, is a heart-pounding adventure that takes you on a rollercoaster ride over the pristine sand dunes. Here's why it's a must-try activity:

- Thrilling Off-Roading: Skilled drivers guide specially equipped 4x4 vehicles through the undulating sand dunes of the Dubai Desert Conservation Reserve. This thrilling experience will have your heart racing as you conquer steep inclines and sharp descents.

- Scenic Views: Dune Bashing offers a unique perspective of Dubai's natural wonders. As you traverse the desert terrain, you'll witness breathtaking panoramas of the rolling dunes stretching as far as the eye can see.

- Sunset Dune Bashing: For a truly magical experience, opt for a sunset dune bashing excursion. Watching the sun dip below the horizon, casting a warm, golden glow over the desert, is a memory you'll cherish forever.

Environmental Conservation:

Dubai takes environmental conservation seriously, and this extends to activities in the desert. Desert Safari and Dune Bashing operators often collaborate with conservation organizations to minimize their impact on the fragile desert ecosystem. Sustainable practices, such as adhering to designated routes and protecting local flora and fauna, are essential aspects of these adventures.

Dubai's natural wonders and outdoor adventures, particularly Desert Safari and Dune Bashing, offer a unique and exhilarating way to explore the stunning desert landscapes that surround this modern metropolis. Whether you seek heart-pounding thrills or tranquil moments in the heart of the Arabian Desert, these experiences promise memories that will last a lifetime. As you embark on these adventures, remember to respect the environment and heritage of this remarkable region, ensuring that future generations can also savor the splendor of Dubai's desert.

Dubai's Pristine Beaches

Dubai, often associated with towering skyscrapers and luxury, is a city that boasts more than just urban opulence. Nestled along the Arabian Gulf, Dubai's pristine beaches offer a remarkable contrast to its modern skyline, serving as an oasis of natural wonders and outdoor adventures. In this article, we will explore the captivating beauty of Dubai's beaches and the diverse range of activities they offer for travelers seeking a harmonious blend of relaxation and adventure.

Golden Sands and Crystal Waters:

Dubai's beaches are renowned for their golden sands and crystal-clear waters. The contrast between the sparkling turquoise sea and the immaculate shores creates a breathtaking sight that draws visitors from around the world. The beaches here are meticulously maintained, making them perfect for sunbathing, beachcombing, or simply enjoying the serene beauty of the coast.

Palm Jumeirah: A Man-Made Wonder:

One of Dubai's most iconic landmarks, the Palm Jumeirah, boasts an array of exclusive beachfront properties and private resorts. The crescent-shaped island offers a unique experience where you can savor the Arabian Gulf on one side and enjoy views of Dubai's skyline on the other. It's a testament to Dubai's architectural prowess, blending seamlessly with the natural beauty of the sea.

Water Sports and Adventure:

Dubai's beaches are not just for leisurely strolls; they are also hubs for adrenaline-pumping water sports. Kite surfing, jet-skiing, parasailing, and windsurfing are just a few of the thrilling activities you can partake in. The warm waters and consistent winds make these beaches ideal for both beginners and seasoned water sports enthusiasts.

Underwater Adventures:

The underwater world around Dubai's beaches is a treasure trove waiting to be explored. Snorkeling and scuba diving enthusiasts can witness vibrant coral reefs teeming with marine life, including colorful fish, turtles, and even the occasional dolphin. The region's diverse marine ecosystem offers a unique opportunity to get up close and personal with the underwater wonders.

Beachfront Dining and Entertainment:

Dubai's beaches aren't just about sun and sea; they also offer a vibrant culinary scene and entertainment options. Many beachfront restaurants and cafes offer delectable international and local cuisine with stunning sea views. As the sun sets, the beaches come alive with beach parties, live music, and cultural performances, providing an enchanting atmosphere for a memorable evening.

Desert Meets Beach:

One of the most distinctive features of Dubai's coastline is the juxtaposition of desert and beach. The golden dunes of the Arabian Desert extend to the very edge of the coastline, creating a surreal and picturesque landscape. Visitors can experience the thrill of desert safaris and camel rides, all within a stone's throw of the pristine beaches.

Conservation and Sustainability:

Dubai is committed to preserving its natural wonders, including its beaches. Various conservation efforts are in place to protect the delicate coastal ecosystems. Travelers can engage in eco-friendly activities such as beach clean-ups and turtle conservation programs, contributing to the sustainable preservation of these stunning natural assets.

Dubai's pristine beaches are more than just a leisure destination; they are a testament to the city's ability to seamlessly blend modernity with nature. With their golden sands, clear waters, and a plethora of activities, Dubai's beaches offer a unique experience for those seeking natural wonders and outdoor adventures. Whether you're a sun-worshipper, a water sports enthusiast, or a nature lover, Dubai's beaches provide an unforgettable escape into the beauty of the Arabian Gulf. So, plan your next adventure to Dubai and discover the harmonious balance of urban sophistication and natural splendor that awaits along its captivating coastline.

Nature Reserves and Parks

Dubai, known for its iconic skyscrapers and modern cityscape, is also a haven for nature enthusiasts and outdoor adventurers. Amidst the urban hustle and bustle, Dubai offers a surprising array of nature reserves and parks that showcase the emirate's diverse natural beauty. In this article, we'll delve into the stunning natural wonders and outdoor adventures that Dubai has to offer through its well-preserved and thoughtfully designed nature reserves and parks.

Dubai Desert Conservation Reserve:

Located in the heart of the desert, the Dubai Desert Conservation Reserve (DDCR) spans over 225 square kilometers, making it the UAE's first national park. This remarkable reserve is dedicated to preserving the unique desert ecosystem and its biodiversity. Visitors can explore the dunes on camelback or in a 4x4 vehicle, experiencing the serene beauty of the desert landscape, which comes to life with the changing colors of sunrise and sunset. It's an ideal place to learn about the local flora and fauna and the Bedouin way of life.

Al Marmoom Desert Conservation Reserve:

Another gem in Dubai's desert landscape, the Al Marmoom Desert Conservation Reserve is one of the largest man-made deserts in the world. This sprawling reserve spans 40 square kilometers and offers a range of outdoor activities, from sandboarding and camel riding to bird watching and stargazing. The reserve's focus on sustainability and conservation ensures that the desert's fragile ecosystem is preserved for future generations.

Dubai Creek Park:

In contrast to the desert reserves, Dubai Creek Park provides a lush green oasis in the heart of the city. Located alongside the historic Dubai Creek, this park offers a serene escape from the urban environment. Visitors can enjoy picnics, pedal boating, and a visit to the Dolphinarium. The park's well-maintained gardens and scenic views of the creek make it a favorite spot for families and nature lovers.

Hatta Mountain Reserve:

Venture beyond the city limits to the Hatta Mountain Reserve, a rugged and picturesque destination nestled in the Hajar Mountains. This reserve is known for its dramatic landscapes, including rocky canyons, natural pools, and hiking trails. The Hatta Dam is a popular spot for kayaking, while the Hatta Wadi Hub offers adventure activities like mountain biking and zip-lining.

Ras Al Khor Wildlife Sanctuary:

Dubai's urban sprawl has not deterred its commitment to wildlife conservation. The Ras Al Khor Wildlife Sanctuary, located at the entrance to Dubai Creek, is home to a variety of bird species, including flamingos, herons, and ospreys. Birdwatchers and nature photographers flock to this sanctuary for its bird hides and informative visitor center.

Dubai Miracle Garden:

For those seeking a more horticultural experience, the Dubai Miracle Garden is a botanical marvel in the heart of the desert. This vibrant garden showcases an array of meticulously designed floral displays, including life-sized structures adorned with colorful blooms. It's a delightful place to explore, particularly during the winter months when the weather is mild.

Dubai's natural wonders and outdoor adventures extend far beyond its gleaming skyscrapers. The city's commitment to preserving its unique ecosystems and creating recreational spaces has led to the development of exceptional nature reserves and parks. Whether you're looking to explore the tranquil desert, relax in a green oasis, or observe wildlife in their natural habitat, Dubai offers a diverse range of outdoor experiences for nature enthusiasts and adventurers alike. These carefully curated destinations showcase Dubai's dedication to sustainability, conservation, and the celebration of its natural heritage.

CHAPTER 6: NAVIGATING DUBAI: PRACTICAL TIPS AND RESOURCES

Transportation and Getting Around

Dubai, the dazzling jewel of the United Arab Emirates, is known for its opulent lifestyle, stunning architecture, and thriving economy. Navigating this dynamic city efficiently is essential, and understanding the transportation options available can greatly enhance your experience. In this comprehensive guide, we provide practical tips and resources for getting around Dubai.

Overview of Dubai's Transportation System

Dubai boasts a modern and extensive transportation infrastructure that makes moving around the city relatively easy. Key components of the city's transportation system include:

1. Dubai Metro

Dubai Metro is the backbone of the city's public transport network. It is clean, efficient, and one of the most convenient ways to get around. The metro has two lines: the Red Line and the Green Line, with numerous stations strategically located throughout the city. It is a great way to avoid traffic and reach key destinations.

2. Public Buses

Public buses cover virtually every corner of Dubai, making them an affordable option for commuting. The buses are air-conditioned and well-maintained, offering a cost-effective way to explore the city.

3. Taxis

Dubai's taxi services are known for their reliability and convenience. You can find taxis easily throughout the city, and they are metered, so there's no need to negotiate fares. The Dubai Taxi Corporation operates a fleet of comfortable vehicles.

4. Dubai Tram

The Dubai Tram primarily serves the Dubai Marina and JBR (Jumeirah Beach Residence) areas. It's a fantastic option for exploring these waterfront communities.

5. *Water Transportation*

Given Dubai's proximity to the Arabian Gulf, water transportation is also an option. You can take an abra (traditional wooden boat) across Dubai Creek or enjoy a more leisurely ride on a water taxi.

Navigating Dubai: Top Practical Tips

1. *Use a Nol Card*

The Nol card is a contactless smart card that allows you to pay for various modes of transportation in Dubai, including the metro, buses, trams, and water taxis. It's more convenient and cost-effective than buying individual tickets.

2. Plan Your Route

Before setting out, use apps like Google Maps or the official RTA Dubai app to plan your journey. These apps provide real-time information on routes, schedules, and estimated travel times.

3. Avoid Rush Hours

Dubai experiences heavy traffic during rush hours, which are typically from 7:30 AM to 9:30 AM and 4:30 PM to 7:00 PM on weekdays. Plan your trips accordingly to avoid congestion.

4. Dress Respectfully

Dubai is a conservative city, so it's advisable to dress modestly when using public transportation.

Avoid clothing that is too revealing, and women should consider covering their shoulders and knees.

5. *Mind the Rules*

Respect local customs and follow the rules when using public transportation. For example, there are designated seating areas for women and families on the metro, and eating or drinking is not allowed on public transport.

Resources for Getting Around Dubai
1. *RTA Dubai Official Website*

The Roads and Transport Authority (RTA) is the government agency responsible for transportation in Dubai. Their website provides comprehensive information on public transportation, including schedules, fares, and route maps.

2. Dubai Metro Map

For a visual guide to the Dubai Metro system, visit the Metro Dubai website. It offers an interactive map and other useful information for metro users.

3. [Careem and Uber Ride-sharing services]

Like Careem and Uber are widely available in Dubai, providing a convenient alternative to traditional taxis.

4. Dubai Transport Apps

The RTA offers a range of mobile apps that can simplify your transportation experience. These apps include the S'hail journey planner and the Smart Taxi app for booking taxis.

Navigating Dubai's transportation system is an integral part of experiencing all that this vibrant city has to offer. By utilizing the resources and following the tips outlined in this guide, you can make your travel in Dubai smooth, efficient, and enjoyable. Whether you're a visitor or a resident, Dubai's well-connected transportation network will ensure you can explore its wonders with ease.

Accommodations for Every Budget

Dubai, the dazzling jewel of the Middle East, beckons travelers with its awe-inspiring skyline, pristine beaches, and a rich blend of cultures. Whether you're a luxury seeker, a mid-range traveler, or a budget-conscious explorer, Dubai offers a wide array of accommodations to suit every budget. In this guide, we'll help you navigate the vibrant city of Dubai, providing practical tips and valuable resources to ensure you find the perfect place to stay, regardless of your budget.

Luxury Living in Dubai:

If you're looking to indulge in opulence, Dubai has a plethora of lavish accommodations to choose from. These upscale hotels offer unparalleled comfort, world-class amenities, and stunning views of the city.

a. Burj Al Arab Jumeirah: Often dubbed the "world's most luxurious hotel," the Burj Al Arab offers extravagant suites, private beaches, and 24/7 personal butler service.

b. Atlantis, The Palm: Located on the Palm Jumeirah, this iconic resort boasts underwater suites, an expansive water park, and over 20 restaurants and bars.

c. The Ritz-Carlton Dubai: This beachfront property offers elegant rooms, a rejuvenating spa, and access to some of Dubai's best golf courses.

Mid-Range Marvels:

Travelers seeking a comfortable yet reasonably priced stay will find a plethora of mid-range options in Dubai. These hotels strike a balance between quality and affordability.

a. Jumeirah Emirates Towers: Offering modern amenities and a central location, this hotel provides a taste of luxury without the extravagant price tag.

b. Movenpick Hotel Jumeirah Beach: Located near the beach, this hotel combines affordability with access to popular attractions and a selection of dining options.

c. Zabeel House by Jumeirah, The Greens: A trendy and stylish hotel, perfect for travelers looking for a vibrant atmosphere without breaking the bank.

Budget-Friendly Stays:

Dubai isn't just for the wealthy; it also caters to budget-conscious travelers. From hostels to guesthouses, you can find comfortable accommodations without overspending.

a. Rove City Centre: This affordable and trendy hotel offers a convenient location and excellent facilities, perfect for budget-conscious travelers.

b. Dubai Youth Hostel: Ideal for backpackers, this hostel provides clean dormitories and a friendly atmosphere while keeping costs low.

c. Arabian Nights Village: For a unique experience, consider staying in a traditional desert camp. It's affordable and provides an authentic taste of Dubai.

Practical Tips for Booking Accommodations in Dubai:

- Book in Advance: Dubai is a popular tourist destination, and accommodations can fill up quickly. Booking in advance ensures you get the best deals.

- Consider Location: Choose accommodations close to your planned activities to save time and transportation costs.

- Use Online Booking Platforms: Websites like Booking.com, Airbnb, and Agoda offer a wide range of options and often have special promotions.

- Check Reviews: Read reviews from previous guests to ensure the quality and reliability of your chosen accommodation.

- Travel During Off-Peak Seasons: Traveling during the shoulder seasons can lead to significant savings on accommodations.

Resources for Finding Accommodations:

- Booking.com: A user-friendly platform offering a vast selection of hotels, apartments, and hostels.
- Airbnb: Ideal for those seeking unique stays, from apartments to villas and even houseboats.
- Agoda: Known for its competitive rates and extensive listings in the Middle East.
- TripAdvisor: A valuable resource for reviews, ratings, and travel recommendations.

Dubai's accommodations cater to travelers of all budgets, ensuring that everyone can experience the city's grandeur and cultural richness. By using practical tips and trusted resources, you can find the perfect place to stay in Dubai, making your trip a memorable and enjoyable experience regardless of your budget constraints. From the heights of luxury to the charms of budget-friendly stays, Dubai has something for every traveler.

Essential Travel Tips and Resources

Dubai, with its iconic skyline, opulent lifestyle, and rich cultural heritage, is a top destination for travelers from around the world. Navigating this vibrant city can be an unforgettable experience, but it's essential to plan and prepare to make the most of your visit. To help you enjoy your Dubai journey to the fullest, we've compiled a comprehensive guide of essential travel tips and resources.

Travel Documents and Visa Requirements

Before you embark on your Dubai adventure, ensure you have the necessary travel documents in order:

Passport: Ensure your passport is valid for at least six months from your planned date of arrival in Dubai.

Visa: Most visitors to Dubai require a visa for entry. Check the visa requirements based on your nationality and purpose of visit. Apply for the appropriate visa well in advance through the official channels or with the assistance of a trusted travel agency.

Best Time to Visit
Dubai experiences a desert climate, with scorching summers and mild winters. To make the most of your trip, consider the following:

November to April: This is the ideal time to visit Dubai when the weather is pleasant, and outdoor activities are enjoyable.

Ramadan: Be aware of Ramadan dates, as some restaurants and attractions may have limited hours during this period.

Accommodation

Dubai offers a wide range of accommodation options to suit all budgets. Here are some considerations:

Location: Choose accommodations based on your interests. If you want to explore historical sites, consider staying in Old Dubai. For a luxurious experience, the Palm Jumeirah or Downtown Dubai may be more suitable.

Booking: Book your accommodation well in advance, especially during peak tourist seasons, to secure the best rates and availability.

Transportation

Getting around Dubai is relatively easy thanks to its modern infrastructure and various transportation options:

Metro: Dubai has an efficient and well-connected metro system. It's a convenient and cost-effective way to travel within the city.

Taxis: Taxis are readily available and are metered. Ensure the driver uses the meter or agree on a fare before starting the ride.

Ride-Sharing Apps: Uber and other ride-sharing apps are widely used in Dubai and offer a convenient alternative to taxis.

Currency and Payments

Dubai's currency is the UAE Dirham (AED). Here's how to manage your finances during your visit:

Currency Exchange: Exchange money at banks, exchange offices, or ATMs for the best rates. Credit and debit cards are widely accepted.

Tipping: While tipping is not mandatory, it is customary to leave a 10-15% tip in restaurants, and it is appreciated for exceptional service.

Local Culture and Etiquette

Respecting the local culture is essential when visiting Dubai:

Dress Code: Dress modestly in public areas, covering shoulders and knees. Swimwear is acceptable at the beach or poolside.

Public Behavior: Public displays of affection, including kissing and hugging, are not tolerated. Be mindful of your behavior in public spaces.

Emergency Contacts

In case of any emergencies, keep these contacts handy:

Police: 999

Ambulance: 998

Fire: 997

Useful Resources

To ensure a smooth and enjoyable visit to Dubai, make use of the following resources:

Dubai Tourism Website: The official tourism website provides up-to-date information on attractions, events, and travel advisories.

Dubai Metro App: Download the Dubai Metro app for real-time updates on train schedules and routes.

Dubai International Airport*:* Familiarize yourself with the airport layout and services before your arrival.

Local SIM Card: Consider purchasing a local SIM card to stay connected and access maps and transportation apps.

Dubai is a city of endless possibilities, and with the right preparation and these essential travel tips and resources in hand, you'll be well-equipped to explore its wonders, from the futuristic skyscrapers to the timeless traditions of the Arabian Gulf. Enjoy your journey to this remarkable destination!

CONCLUSION

In concluding this comprehensive Dubai Travel Guide for the years 2024-2025, we find ourselves not merely at the end of a book, but at the threshold of an extraordinary journey. Dubai, the Jewel of the Middle East, continues to captivate and inspire travelers from around the world with its unrivaled blend of tradition and innovation, culture and modernity, and natural beauty and architectural marvels.

As we have journeyed through the pages of this guide, we have sought to provide you, the discerning traveler, with a deep and multifaceted understanding of Dubai's essence. It is a city where the past is honored with reverence, where the present is celebrated with grandeur, and where the future is envisioned with limitless ambition.

In the process of exploring Dubai, we have uncovered the captivating stories of its history, from its humble beginnings as a fishing village to its meteoric rise as a global hub for business, tourism, and culture. We have delved into the diverse neighborhoods and districts that make up this sprawling metropolis, each with its unique charm and character. From the historic lanes of Old Dubai to the glitzy skyscrapers of the Marina, Dubai offers something for every traveler.

Our exploration of Dubai's cultural tapestry has revealed a city that is both a melting pot of international influences and a steadfast guardian of its Emirati heritage. We have savored the flavors of traditional Emirati cuisine, marveled at the calligraphy and craftsmanship of local artisans, and reveled in the lively festivals that showcase Dubai's rich cultural diversity.

Dubai's natural beauty has also been a focal point of our journey. The pristine beaches, the vast desert dunes, and the serene oases have offered respite and reflection amidst the urban bustle. Whether you are seeking adventure, relaxation, or a bit of both, Dubai's natural landscapes provide the perfect backdrop.

Of course, Dubai's iconic skyline and cutting-edge architecture cannot be overlooked. The city's commitment to pushing the boundaries of design and innovation is evident in every gleaming skyscraper, and we have explored some of the most iconic landmarks, including the Burj Khalifa, Palm Jumeirah, and the Dubai Mall.

As we conclude this travel guide, we hope that you are not only equipped with practical information for your visit but also inspired to embark on your own exploration of this dynamic and enchanting city. Dubai is a place where dreams are realized, and possibilities are limitless, making it a destination like no other.

Remember that Dubai is more than just a destination; it is an experience, a journey, and an adventure waiting to unfold. Embrace the culture, savor the cuisine, relish the experiences, and immerse yourself in the grandeur that is Dubai. Your voyage to the Jewel of the Middle East in 2024-2025 promises to be an unforgettable chapter in your travel story.

May your stay in Dubai be filled with discovery, wonder, and cherished memories. Safe travels, and may your Dubai adventure be as magnificent as the city itself.

Printed in Great Britain
by Amazon

32190577R00086